PRENTICE HALL
professional educator's library

HOW ◆ TO ASSESS STUDENT WORK

Lida Lim

ABOUT THE AUTHOR

Lida Lim began teaching in 1961 and retired in 1995. She taught seventh/eighth grade language arts, social studies, and Spanish at Burlingame Intermediate School in Burlingame, California, and served as the advisory coordinator from 1981-1995. She is currently an educational consultant to the Burlingame School District. Co-author of both a spelling and a language arts program, Ms. Lim is a faculty member of the California League of Middle Schools/High Schools Academic Program and a trainer, consultant, and mentor in schools and school districts. She works with first- and second-year teachers and consults on topics such as assessment, teaming, and school culture, as well as her first love, language arts. She brings strong experience in program development and curriculum planning to her work with Prentice Hall.

ACKNOWLEDGMENTS

Writing this book was not a singular effort. I had help. I collaborated with a colleague, Kathy Tuchman Glass, who was of immense assistance. Kathy spent countless hours working with me on the portfolio section of this book. A number of colleagues from Burlingame Intermediate School in California contributed specific assignments. I thank the following colleagues for their creativity and contributions: Carryl Breon, Linda Garrow, Geri Greenlee, Angela House, Donna Morris, May Neupauer, and Lily Ning. To my editors, Kathleen Manatt and Paula Preller, how patient you were in working through the manuscript and offering countless ways to improve what was written, thank you.

Editor: Paula Hansen Preller
Design and Page Composition: Siren design Inc.
Cover Design: Suzanne Schineller
Cover Photo: Rich Iwasaki/Tony Stone Images

Prentice Hall

Printed in the United States of America.
    7 8 9 10   03 02 01 00 99

ISBN: 0-13-433908-8

Table of Contents

Introduction   1

| Part 1 | Integrating Instruction and Assessment | 5 |

Assessment Tools   7

Observing, Discussing, and Listening Beforehand   8

    Observing and Listening to a Student Discussion   9

Using a Video to Assess Student Understanding   10

    Video Viewing Guide   11

Paper-and-Pencil Testing   12

    Computer Vocabulary Test Jeopardy Style   13

Using Bloom's Taxonomy for Assessment   14

    Assessment Vocabulary Based on Bloom's Taxonomy   15

      Science Test   16

Student Products   18

    Possible Products   19

Planning Student Products   20

    Product Planning Form   21

Developing Assignment Sheets that Lead to Student Products   22

    At the Sound of the Beep   23

Language Arts and Social Studies Assignment Sheet   24

    African Environmental Poetry   25

ESL Assignment Sheet   26

    Twentieth Century Exhibit   27

Math Assignment Sheet   28

    How Much Is One Million?   29

Science Assignment Sheet   30

    Marble Racers Letter   31

      The Challenge: Marble Racers   32

        Scoring for Marble Racers 34

Part 2	**Using Rubrics**	**35**
	The Rubric	37
	☑ A Super Rubric for Assessing Work Performance	39
	Levels of Performance	40
	☑ Quality of Performance for a Six-Level Rubric	41
	Generic Rubrics	42
	☑ A Generic Rubric	43
	The Language of Rubrics: Performance Descriptors	44
	◄ A Variety of Performance Descriptors	45
	The Language of Rubrics: Areas to Be Evaluated	46
	◄ Areas to Be Evaluated in Semi-Generic Rubrics	47
	Rubrics for Project Work	48
	☑ A Rubric for Project Work	49
	Rubrics for Group Work	50
	☑ Measure Your Success	51
	Specific Rubrics	52
	☑ A Rubric for Listening Skills	53
	Language Arts Writing Rubric	54
	☑ A Rubric for Writing	55
	Rubric for a Performance	56
	✎ *The Pearl*	57
	☑ Rubric for *The Pearl*	58
	Math Problems	59
	✎ Math Problem of the Week: A Strange Tug-of-War	60
	☑ Math Problem of the Week Rubric	61
	✎ Performance-Based Math Task	62
	☑ Rubric for Scoring Performance-Based Math Task	63
	Science Project	64
	✎ Invertebrate Newspaper Project	65
	☑ Invertebrate Newspaper Evaluation	67
	Rubric for an Oral Presentation	68
	✎ Newspaper Presentation	69
	☑ Newspaper Presentation Evaluation Form	70
	☑ Newspaper Presentation Rubric	72
	Creating Rubrics	73
	☑ Your Rubric for Chocolate Chip Cookies	75
	☑ Another Rubric for Chocolate Chip Cookies	76

Part 3	Establishing a Portfolio Program	77
	Purposes of Portfolios	79
	Examples of Learning Processes Shown by Specific Products	81
	Purposes of Portfolios	83
	Setting up a Portfolio Program	84
	Planning Guide	86
	Selecting the Contents of the Portfolio	87
	Portfolio Guidelines for Students	88
	A Letter to Parents at the Beginning of the Year	90
	A Letter to Parents at the End of the Portfolio Process	91
	Portfolio Contents	92
	Portfolio Contents	93
	Content Reflection	94
	Content Reflection	95
	Reader Comment Page	96
	Reader Comment Page	97
	Teacher Comment Page	98
	Teacher Comment Page	99
	Choosing Content Pieces	100
	Portfolio Checklist: Criteria for a Complete Portfolio	101
	Sharing Portfolios	103
	Managing a Portfolio Program	104
	Teacher and Student Roles in the Portfolio Process	105
	Evaluating Portfolios	106
	A Rubric for Evaluating My Portfolio	107
	Teacher Self-Reflection	108
	Self-Reflection on My Portfolio Program	109
	Some Questions to Ask Yourself about Portfolio Assessment	110
	Some Questions to Ask Yourself about Portfolio Assessment	111
Glossary of Terms		**113**

INTRODUCTION

*To know that you know what you know
and that you do not know what you do not know
that is true knowledge*

—Confucius

As educators, we've experienced many progressive changes in the last several years: new curriculum standards and frameworks, new teaching strategies, and new technology, to name a few. Teachers are moving away from being the "sage on the stage" by delivering discrete bits of information. Instead we are becoming the "guide on the side" by facilitating the learning of students in an integrated, active, reflective learning environment. When such a fundamental shift in instructional strategies takes place, a traditional approach to assessment just doesn't work anymore. We discover that the paper-and-pencil tests that use to characterize all our formal assessments don't accurately reflect all the teaching and learning going on in our classrooms.

We can learn something by looking at what many would consider teenagers' favorite assessment: the driving test. In order to receive their licenses, teenagers must prove they are qualified to drive by taking a paper-and-pencil test and giving a behind-the-wheel demonstration of their driving abilities. They are tested on what they are taught and what they are expected to learn. They know beforehand exactly what is expected and how they are going to be assessed. Such principles can form the basis of a successful classroom assessment program.

Learning how to design assessments that accurately reflect what and how students have been taught isn't learned in a day. I have spent years learning more about this topic. When I realized that I needed to change the way I assessed students' work, I began reading professional articles and books. I attended conferences highlighting authentic assessment and asked my administration for staff development in this area. I then took the new ideas I was learning and turned them into actual classroom assignments, tests, and practices. I found that my assessments were becoming more useful to the students and their parents, as well as to me. In fact, assessing actually became easier. And I hope that as you use this book, you'll find the same thing.

This is an interactive book. It offers explanations, guiding questions, planning forms, and many successful examples of assessment practices, most of which can simply be photocopied and used. The book consists of three parts that each discuss a key element of a successful classroom assessment program:

Part 1: Integrating Instruction and Assessment

Part 2: Using Rubrics

Part 3: Establishing a Portfolio Program

Part 1 gives many examples of how to integrate classroom instruction and assessment. It looks at ways to turn instructional strategies into testing strategies. It shows that you don't have to throw out paper-and-pencil testing altogether but that you can find appropriate and creative ways to ensure that these tests are aligned with the way you are teaching. You'll find activities showing that listening to students' discussions and observing their work habits are an important and natural part of the assessment process. There is also a major section on student products. I am a firm believer in student products as a major form of assessment. These products include journal writing, audio and/or video tapes, demonstrations, dramatic performances, visual displays, debates, investigations, simulations, physical constructions, and role playing scenarios. Products such as these enable students to participate in high-level learning. The classroom atmosphere becomes engaging and active, and students feel a strong sense of self-satisfaction upon completion of their products.

I can recall times when after collecting students' completed products I'd ask myself, "How am I going to grade this?" I devised both simple and complicated point systems and check-off sheets that seemed to satisfy most students. However, there were those who wanted to know why they received 8 points instead of 10. They wanted to know what they could do to make their products better, and more importantly, why I hadn't specified beforehand exactly what they had to do to earn the full ten points. I thought I had. But what I had failed to do was define and describe what 10 points looked like. This was an area of assessment that needed clarification. And this is when I began to discover what a valuable assessment tool a rubric could be. As you'll see in Part 2, "Using Rubrics," rubrics show students the specific levels of performance that are expected and how their work will be evaluated. Part 2 gives step-by-step guidelines for creating original rubrics, and it also includes numerous examples of successful rubrics that can be used as is or adapted to fit specific needs.

Part 3, "Establishing a Portfolio Program," discusses how and why to set up a portfolio program. Portfolios are a powerful tool for self-reflection. It's not just teachers that need to assess — students do too. In my classroom, I had always included peer response to student work. Students worked hard at helping each other and their responses were, indeed, constructive. But one day, I happened to ask students to write a note telling me how they, themselves, thought they did on their projects. I was absolutely amazed at their responses. The learning that took place during this self-reflection was extremely valuable. I began to realize the power of self-reflection as an assessment tool. The enhancement to self-esteem was also clear. I saw that portfolios of student work provided a meaningful resource for student self-reflection. The "old student folders" in my room became a systematic portfolio procedure which proved more effective in allowing students to see the progress they had made. Part 3 includes many instructions and forms that can be used when developing a portfolio program.

The models and forms presented in *How to Assess Student Work* are classroom tested and have provided me and my colleagues at the Burlingame Intermediate School with many enriching assessment experiences. I hope this book will help and encourage you in your assessment practices as well. I'd love to hear *your* success stories!

Lida Lim

Integrating Instruction and Assessment

ASSESSMENT TOOLS

Integrating instruction and assessment is natural. After all, one of the main reasons we assess is so that we'll know what needs to be instructed. We assess before, during, and after we instruct so that we can keep shaping our instruction to match students' needs. Before long, instruction and assessment should be so well integrated they become virtually indistinguishable.

In this section you'll find many assessment tools to use before, during, and after instruction. The sample ideas shown provide many creative ways to collect the kind of data you need for assessing student learning. You'll see examples of how to reap useful information from student discussions that take place before a new unit is begun. There are also samples of successful paper-and-pencil tests. For example, the science test on pages 16 and 17 really makes students think, and it was extremely popular with the students who took it.

Giving students the opportunity to create a unique product that shows what they know and can do is a keystone to any assessment program. You will find many ideas about how to go about assigning and helping students plan and complete such products. These products accurately reflect the teaching and learning going on in the classroom, and, as a result, they are fair and fun ways to assess what students have learned.

As you'll see in this section, effective programs include assessments that:

- emphasize production instead of one right answer
- stress self-evaluation
- look at work in progress
- reflect good instructional practices
- use a variety of ways to collect data
- encourage student judgment not just memory
- show what students can do, rather than what they cannot do.

OBSERVING, DISCUSSING, AND LISTENING BEFOREHAND

Listening to student discussion before starting a unit of study is extremely useful. It can help you design the curriculum. It shows you what students know already, know incorrectly, and don't yet know. This is essential information for developing effective and engaging curriculum. These discussions can also assist you in forming heterogeneous groups for studying a specific topic.

When introducing a new topic of study, present it in the form of a question or a direction:

- What do you know about _____ ?
- Talk about _____ .

"Listen" to the student conversation on the next page. Then draw some instructional conclusions that will help you design a unit of study. Next, pair off the students from the discussion based on what they have stated. Obviously, in your own classroom you will be able to use the knowledge you have about individual students' work habits, learning styles, and skills to help you form student groupings. However, for this scenario, determine these pairings based on what you "hear."

Observing and Listening to a Student Discussion

Teacher: "What do you know about electricity?"

Chris: "We use electricity for almost everything."

Leonard: "Animals don't use electricity. They don't need it."

Jan: "Electricity isn't really a thing, like something you touch; it's more like a force that makes things work."

Jared: "Electricity is made at hydroelectric plants. I saw one at Hoover Dam last summer."

Dale: "Some dams cause problems for the fish and other animals that live at the river."

Josh: "Beavers make dams, too."

Alicia: "I can make static electricity by rubbing my feet along the carpet and then touching something like a doorknob. Want to see?"

Laurel: "No! So, Jan's not right, you can touch electricity. You don't want to touch it though because it's dangerous, like lightning. Lightning is a big spark of electricity."

1. What instructional conclusions can you reach based on this conversation that will help you design a unit of study on electricity?

_____

_____

_____

2. Which students would you pair up?

a. _____ _____

b. _____ _____

c. _____ _____

d. _____ _____

USING A VIDEO TO ASSESS STUDENT UNDERSTANDING

Showing a video is one way to introduce a unit or to present information on a specific topic. One technique that will help you assess how much information your class brings to the topic is to show five minutes of the video with the sound muted. Divide the class into small groups. As the class watches the muted video, encourage the groups to:

- talk about what they are seeing
- talk about their reactions to what they are seeing
- talk about the factual content of the video
- formulate questions they want answered as they are viewing the video.

Next, replay the five-minute video segment with the sound on. In their groups, the students can now compare their earlier discussions to what they now know from hearing the audio. This can be followed by individual written responses to the question, "What did you learn from this activity?" You can use the form on the next page for this activity.

Video Viewing Guide

1. Write down words, feelings, and thoughts that come to mind as you watch the video with the sound muted.

_____

_____

_____

2. What questions would you like to have answered once the sound is on?

_____

_____

_____

3. Write down words, feelings, and thoughts that come to mind as you watch the video with the sound on.

_____

_____

_____

4. Write down answers to your questions in number 2 above.

_____

_____

_____

5. What did you learn from this activity?

_____

_____

_____

6. What would you like to learn about this topic? What questions do you still have about this topic?

_____

_____

_____

PAPER-AND-PENCIL TESTING

It is important that we do not abandon paper-and-pencil testing altogether, as it is important that we not abandon direct instruction. Sometimes direct instruction is the most effective way to teach material. If we want students to know specific information through direct instruction, then we need to test them directly to assess how well they have learned this information. If we want students to know the capitals of the states, then we test directly for this knowledge. However, it does not have to be a traditional paper-and-pencil test.

We can use an instructional strategy as an assessment tool. Many of us use games to motivate students to learn. We can assess in the same way, for example, by using a game format to test vocabulary. On the next page, you'll find a computer class vocabulary test modeled after the television game "Jeopardy." There are 90 possible points on this test. You will need to devise a scoring guide, such as the one suggested here:

81-90 = A

72-80 = B

63-71 = C

54-62 = D

Computer Vocabulary Test
Jeopardy Style

On the Jeopardy board below you will find basic computer terms. They are the answers. You need to supply the *questions*. You will receive points for each correct question you write in the lines below. Look at the top of the column to see the number of points you'll earn for giving the correct question for an answer.

5	10	15
1. back-up	4. hard copy	7. bit
2. disk	5. file	8. font
3. graphics	6. modem	9. CPU

WHAT IS THE QUESTION?

1. (5 points) _____

2. (5 points) _____

3. (5 points) _____

4. (10 points) _____

5. (10 points) _____

6. (10 points) _____

7. (15 points) _____

8. (15 points) _____

9. (15 points) _____

USING BLOOM'S TAXONOMY FOR ASSESSMENT

We want to help students become good reasoners, independent thinkers, and clear communicators. Then when we establish standards, develop curriculum, and determine instructional strategies, we need to be sure to include material that requires high-level thinking skills. Bloom's Taxonomy of the Cognitive Domain can be a useful tool in our work. You may remember that in 1956 Benjamin Bloom outlined six levels of cognitive function: knowledge, comprehension, application, analysis, synthesis, and evaluation. His taxonomy has been taught to and used by educators ever since. When developing curriculum and determining instruction, we look at these six levels and think of them in terms of action verbs, as you can see in the second column of the chart on the next page.

As teachers, we've tended to overlook how helpful this taxonomy can be when it comes to assessing student understanding. We can use the taxonomy as a guide when we are developing tests or student projects. The third column of the chart on the next page lists words and phrases that can be used when creating tests or projects. Pages 16-17 show an example of a test that follows Bloom's taxonomy.

Assessment Vocabulary Based on Bloom's Taxonomy

COGNITIVE DOMAIN	DESCRIPTIVE VERBS	ASSESSMENT WORDS/PHRASES
Knowledge	List, Describe, Catalog, Itemize, Define, Classify, Organize, Identify, Name, Show, Indicate, Explain, Read	Who, What, Where, When, Why, How, How much, Which one Describe… Select…
Comprehension	Change, Infer, Outline, Propose, Replace, Modify, Summarize, Alter, Vary, Condense, Explain	Which are facts/opinions? What does this mean? Outline the information in… Restate in your own words… Explain what is happening… Summarize…
Application	Solve, Predict, Explain, Diagnose, Estimate, Plan, Project, Judge	What would happen if… Explain the effects of… What and how much would change…
Analysis	Examine, Compare, Contrast, Identify, Equate, Rank, Deduce	What conclusions can be drawn from… What is the theme or main idea? What is the relationship… Which are the most important ideas? What is the motive of…
Synthesis	Create, Brainstorm, Predict, Plan, Design, Set up, Imagine	Make up, Choose, Create, Design, Plan
Evaluation	Judge, Rank, Determine, Critique, Defend, Conclude	Which is more important/ moral/logical/appropriate/ valid? Compare and contrast… Critique…

Science Test

Select the questions you wish to answer. You must select questions so that they add up to 100 points. You cannot select more or fewer than 100 points.

Knowledge (5 points each)

1. Whose atomic model was referred to as "plum pudding"?

2. Which atomic particle has a negative charge?

3. Which atomic particle orbits the nucleus?

Comprehension (10 points each)

1. Name two physical properties of metals.

2. Diagram a Bohr model of the atom nitrogen.

3. Using a periodic chart, identify five metals and five nonmetals.

Application (15 points each)

1. Explain how to test for the presence of oxygen.

2. Using a periodic chart, determine how many valence electrons can be found in astatine.

3. Given the three elements, Na, Cl, and Ne, predict which two will form a compound.

Analysis (20 points each)

1. Compare an acidic solution with a basic solution.

2. Using a periodic chart, identify these elements as either metals, nonmetals, or metalloids: Na, Cu, Ag, Si, Ge, C, O, Ne, Ar.

3. Compare and contrast the properties of gold with the properties of carbon. Your answer should include five similarities and five differences.

Synthesis (25 points each)

1. Tell me how you could explain the "rule of eight" (bonding) to a fifth grade student. What analogy would you use? Pretend I am the fifth grade student. Write what you would say and do.

2. Design and create a new element. It should include the following information: name, symbol, atomic number, mass number, and number of protons, electrons, and neutrons. Describe its properties.

3. Create a simple poem to describe any element of your choice. Include at least six descriptors.

Source: Linda Garrow, Science Teacher, Burlingame Intermediate School

STUDENT PRODUCTS

There are many ways to assess student understanding other than paper-and-pencil testing. Assigning student projects that lead to final products is rewarding for teachers and students. These products provide students the opportunity to:

- demonstrate what they know in a unique and attractive way
- display their creativity and originality
- do thoughtful work
- show initiative
- work independently and/or within a group
- interact and cooperate with others.

In addition, these products can:

- motivate the reluctant student
- provide memorable activities for students
- integrate skills and knowledge from other subject areas.

You will find a list of possible products on the next page. This list can be reproduced for students to keep in their binders. Once a student selects one of the suggested products and completes it, the product is crossed off her/his list and cannot be repeated. In this way, students are forced to experience variety rather than stay with a familiar, tried-and-true product.

Possible Products

Advertisement	Editorial	Notebook
Article	Essay	Pamphlet
Artwork	Exhibit	Photo Essay
Audiotape	Experiment	Poem
Book	Flashcards	Poster
Chart	Game	Report
Collage	Graph	Scrapbook
Collection	How-to-Manual	Script
Composition	HyperCard® Stack	Skit
Debate	Impersonation	Song
Design	Interview	Speech
Diagram	Journal	Story
Dialogue	Map	Survey
Diary	Model	Timeline
Display	Mural	Transparency
Drawing	Newspaper	Videotape

PLANNING STUDENT PRODUCTS

When assigning student products, it is important to keep a few guidelines in mind. First, provide students with a list of multiple products to consider, such as the list on the previous page. Then, be sure to give students some kind of format for planning their products so that they can set specific goals, anticipate their needs, and organize their efforts before they get started. Insist that students show you their plans before they begin their work. It's also helpful to give them an opportunity to think about how their work will be evaluated before they begin. Lastly, make sure that you provide sufficient project time in the class schedule so that students will have enough time to complete quality products.

When you assign group projects, keep in mind how difficult it can be for students to get together after school or on weekends. Too often out-of-school group projects result in one person doing all the work. Therefore, insisting that all group work be done in class helps to avoid this problem.

On the following page you will find a product planning form. You can have students use this form to plan their projects or devise one of your own.

Product Planning Form

This form is designed to help you get organized before you begin work on your product. You must complete this form and show it to me before you begin your work.

Name: _____ Class period: _____

Begin work on: _____

Complete work on: _____

Topic: _____

My product is: _____

1. This is what I hope to learn from this product:

_____

2. This is a short description of my product:

_____

_____

3. I will use the following resources: (circle each resource you think you will use)

books   interviews   polls   newspapers

magazines   audiotapes   videotapes   Internet

computer research programs   other _____

4. Problems I might encounter while completing my product:

_____

5. Assistance I will need from others to complete my product:

_____

6. I think my product should be evaluated in this way:

_____

7. I expect to get this grade on my product: _____

DEVELOPING ASSIGNMENT SHEETS THAT LEAD TO STUDENT PRODUCTS

There are many occasions when you want to assign the entire class a specific product to create, and therefore the Product Planning Form on the previous page is too generic. A specific student assignment sheet is what you need instead.

Student assignment sheets specify exactly what you are asking the students to produce. They spell out in detail:

- what the student must do
- what the product should contain
- how the product will be evaluated.

Sometimes they include a schedule of due dates or outline in order the steps the students should take to complete the products. In all cases, they provide a written copy of exactly what the teacher is expecting.

On the following pages, 23-34, you will find samples of several specific student assignment sheets. They can be used as models or straight out of the book.

LANGUAGE ARTS ASSIGNMENT SHEET

"At the Sound of the Beep" was developed for a class that had studied the Salem Witch Trials, watched the PBS video "Three Sovereigns for Sarah," and read *Sarah Bishop* by Scott O'Dell. The assignment provided students with a fun opportunity to demonstrate how well they knew the characters, including their motives and speech patterns. Students also demonstrated how accurately they understood this particular period in history. This assignment can be adapted to any novel, to any time period in history, or even to scientific concepts by having one scientist talk to another scientist. It can easily serve as an interdisciplinary activity.

At the Sound of the Beep

PURPOSE: To show that you understand the time period and the characters from our study of the Salem Witch Trials, *Sarah Bishop,* and "Three Sovereigns for Sarah"

PRODUCT: Answering machine messages — a written script and an audiotape

PROCEDURE: Imagine that during the time of the Salem Witch Trials and of *Sarah Bishop,* both telephones and answering machines were available. Given this scenario, you are to do the activities described below with a partner.

1. Create an answering machine message as a "main character" from the historical materials you have read, *Sarah Bishop,* or "Three Sovereigns for Sarah." What message might we hear if we called that person?

2. Select three other characters from your study and create the messages that they would leave "at the sound of the beep."

3. You are to write the script and actually tape your messages, and you are required to turn in both the audiotape and the script.

EVALUATION: You will be graded on originality, quality of content, proper diction, word choice, and enunciation.

LANGUAGE ARTS AND SOCIAL STUDIES ASSIGNMENT SHEET

The following assignment sheet asks students to complete a product using material learned from social studies and language arts. It was used in a class that was a combination of two subjects, language arts and social studies, taught by one teacher during a block of time. The students were studying poetry and the geography of the African continent. The teacher explained to the students that when writing poems about a particular area, they must use their imaginations to feel, see, touch, and hear the area. Their poems, then, would show whether they truly understood the geography of the area. This assignment required the students to work both individually and in cooperative groups of four.

In order to use this activity, you need to provide examples of different types of poetry. You also need to ensure that a variety of art supplies are available.

African Environmental Poetry

PURPOSE: To write a poem about what it is like in a certain area of Africa

PRODUCT: In your cooperative groups you will create a poster containing: a title, four poems, and graphics. Each group member is responsible for writing one poem and designing a graphic to accompany this poem.

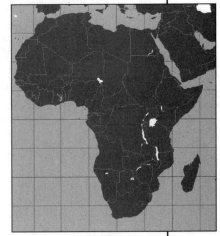

PROCEDURE: If you follow these steps, you will be successful.

1. As a group:
   - select an environment: desert, rain forest, semi-arid, or savanna
   - select a theme such as: animals, vegetation, weather, water, sights, sounds, tastes, colors
   - decide how your final product will look and who will do each part of putting it together, such as printing the title and pasting the poems and graphics.

2. Individual responsibilities:
   - study the poetry types and samples
   - choose the type of poetry you would like to write
   - study your class notes on the environment you selected
   - list ideas and words that you might use in your poem
   - write a first draft of your poem
   - read the draft aloud to yourself and/or to your group
   - ask for suggestions on your poem from your group members
   - edit your poem
   - make a final copy
   - design and complete your graphic.

3. When your group planning and individual responsibilities are completed, you are ready as a group to create your final product. Work diligently and carefully so that your final product is one that you are proud to display in the classroom.

EVALUATION: You will be graded on the use of descriptive language in your poems, how well you incorporated research information, and the neatness of the final poster.

Source: Carryl Breon, Social Studies/Language Arts Teacher, Burlingame Intermediate School

ESL ASSIGNMENT SHEET

The following assignment was given in an English as a second language class. The teacher had scheduled a field trip to the Egyptian section of a local museum. In discussing this trip with the students, the teacher discovered they did not understand the word *exhibit*. She then assigned the following product in order to clarify the word *exhibit* and to prepare her students for the field trip.

Twentieth Century Exhibit

PURPOSE: To understand the word *exhibit*

PRODUCT: An exhibit

PROCEDURE: Do steps 1, 2, and 3 at home. We will do steps 4 and 5 in class. Please do not do them at home.

1. Think of an important object or thing that we use today. Then pick an object that you know about. You may use the actual object or make a model of it for your exhibit.

2. Put your object into a box for showing. You can make a box out of cardboard if you do not have one.

3. Find or draw a picture of someone using your object.

4. Write three paragraphs about your object:
   - describe what it is made of
   - describe how it works
   - explain why we need it.

5. When everyone has completed steps 1 to 4, we will put all our boxes together and make an exhibit.

EVALUATION: You will be graded on how accurately your three paragraphs describe your object and on whether your work at home and in class shows that you understand the term, *exhibit*.

Remember the object you choose should be an important one from the Twentieth Century. Have fun!

Source: May Louise Neupauer, ESL Teacher, Burlingame Intermediate School

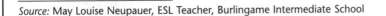

MATH ASSIGNMENT SHEET

The following math assignment results in very creative and interesting posters. Before the teacher gave this assignment, she provided many opportunities in class for the students to do mini-experiments with the number, one million, similar to those specified in the assignment sheet. For example, the class figured out how many miles long a line of a million one dollar bills would stretch and how many bags of beans it would take to total one million individual beans. The students were then able to complete the assignment on their own. This student product easily shows how well students understand the concept of one million.

How Much Is One Million?

PURPOSE: To show what 1,000,000 represents

PRODUCT: Marvelous Million Poster

PROCEDURE: Complete the four tasks below and then show your results in a poster. You may work individually or with a partner.

Task 1 — One Million in Time:
How long does it take to do something one million times? For example, how many hours, days, weeks, or years would it take for you to recite a tongue twister or read aloud a page in a book one million times?

Task 2 — Measuring One Million:
Choose an object, such as a jeep or a stairstep. Then figure out how many miles long a line of one million of those objects would stretch.

Task 3 — Counting One Million:
Choose a small item that usually comes in groups and calculate how many groups would equal one million of the item. For example, how many cookies equal one million chocolate chips; how many boxes of rice equal one million grains of rice?

Task 4 — Counting One Million Words:
Figure out how many pages or books would equal one million words. For example, one million names covers how many pages in a phone book; one million words takes up how many pages in a newspaper?

5. Making a Marvelous Million Poster:
Present your findings in a poster. It should be 18" x 24" and include typed explanations as well as illustrations or photographs for each task. Follow the format below for each task:

- Question: (task stated in the form of a question)
- My Guess: (do this before you do any experimenting with numbers)
- Solution: (this is the answer to the question)
- Process: (Give a detailed, step-by-step explanation of how you arrived at your solution. You may use a calculator but record the numbers and operations you used to arrive at your solutions.)

EVALUATION: You will be graded on accuracy, clarity, completeness, and neatness.

Source: Geri Greenlee, Math/Language Arts Teacher, Burlingame Intermediate School

SCIENCE ASSIGNMENT SHEET

On pages 31-34, you will find several forms involving a major science project. Students demonstrate that they understand the concepts they learned in a physical science class by constructing a marble racetrack. The work is completed at home, so it is important to elicit the help of students' parents or guardians. On the following page you will find a letter home explaining the project and describing the help needed.

Pages 32-33 outline the assignment. The project requires a significant amount of time, so a schedule has been included to help students keep on track. In addition, the assignment sheet indicates specific point values for each step of the project, which gives students the opportunity to control how well they will perform on the assignment. This incorporates the idea that student expectations are an important aspect of designing meaningful assessments. Finally, page 34 includes the form the teachers used to assess the final product.

Marble Racers Letter

Dear Students and Parents/Guardians:

It is time to begin work on this year's Challenge. The science teachers have coordinated this project so that all students will have the same challenge. This year's challenge pertains to physics and engineering.

The Challenge
Design a device that will allow a marble to remain in motion for as close to two minutes as possible. The marble must take at least four changes in direction.

We see science as an opportunity to solve problems creatively. This particular problem involves hands-on application of knowledge the students have learned in class. There are opportunities for teamwork and collaboration.

Enclosed is information about the "Marble Racer" project and a schedule outlining important due dates to help students pace themselves with the work. Students should not wait until the last minute!

Consider that during the next three weeks, students will have daily homework on some aspect of the project. Parents/Guardians: You can help with this by checking your student's progress periodically.

We are looking forward to working with you to make this a valuable learning experience for your child, and we appreciate your support on this important project.

Sincerely,

Linda Garrow and Angela House, Science Teachers

The Challenge: Marble Racers

PURPOSE: To design and construct a device that allows a marble to remain in motion for exactly two minutes and take at least four changes in direction

PRODUCT: Marble Racetrack

PROCEDURE: You may work as an individual or in pairs as you complete the steps below. The number of points in parentheses shows the total number of points you can receive for each part of the project. A perfect score for the complete project is 600 points.

1. Design and construct a racetrack.   (200 points)

   The racetrack should:

   • keep the marble in motion for as close to two minutes (120 seconds) as possible

   • use three different simple machines

   • force the marble to change direction at least four times

   • not require hands, batteries, or electricity to move the marble.

2. Write a project summary.   (200 points)

   It must be typed and list the project title and the names of the project members. Your summary must also include a paragraph on each of these items:

   • how group got started; where idea originated

   • how device works; what keeps it in motion

   • how it was built

   • problems encountered; solutions implemented

   • acknowledgments — people who helped

   • reflection — what happened on the day of the challenge.

3. Draw a diagram of the racetrack.   (200 points)

   • Make a full color drawing of the racetrack using colored pencils or markers on 8 1/2" x 11" paper.

   • Use labels to indicate the type of materials used.

   • Include arrows and footnotes to show the path of the marble, and use numbers to mark where the marble changes direction.

   • Include names of project members and title of your project.

GUIDELINES:

1. Your teacher will provide the marble on the day of the challenge.

2. Use household or purchased materials to construct your racetrack. You should not have to buy all new materials.

3. On the day of the challenge, you will be allowed a maximum time of five minutes to set up your racetrack.

PROJECT DUE DATES:

First Week: Introduce project, select partners, do research on simple machines

Second Week: Design the racetrack, purchase any needed materials

Third Week: Build the racetrack, try out the racetrack, make any needed modifications

Fourth Monday: Day of the Challenge — projects due for judging

Source: Linda Garrow and Angela House, Science Teachers, Burlingame Intermediate School

Scoring for Marble Racers

PROJECT REQUIREMENTS	YOUR POINTS	MAXIMUM POINTS
1. The Racetrack		
A) Amount of time in motion: 1 point per second; minus one point for each second over 120 seconds, even if marble is off the track	_____	120
B) Number of different simple machines: 20 points for each different simple machine	_____	60
C) Number of changes in direction: 5 points for each change in direction	_____	20
2. Project Summary:		
A) All 6 paragraphs included: 20 points for each required paragraph	_____	120
B) Mechanics and neatness	_____	40
C) Content	_____	40
3. Diagram:		
A) Marble path properly marked	_____	50
B) Accuracy of diagram	_____	100
C) Neatness	_____	50
Total Points	_____	600

Source: Linda Garrow and Angela House, Science Teachers, Burlingame Intermediate School

Using Rubrics

PART 2

THE RUBRIC

A rubric is a guide that gives direction to the scoring of student products. It is especially helpful for assessing products such as open-ended questions, lab experiments, debates, oral presentations, visual representations, and written work.

Usually presented in chart form, rubrics describe various levels of work performance. They identify specific characteristics to look for when assessing whether a particular product or performance is good, very good, or not good enough.

In an active classroom, rubrics are an integral part of formal assessment. They are a very useful tool for evaluating subjective assignments with objective consistency. Rubrics can also help teachers visualize the final products they assign. They encourage teachers to determine specifically what is expected at various levels of performance rather than just what is expected at the "A" level. As teachers think through the various responses and performances resulting from assignments, they can anticipate where problem areas might arise when students are executing the assignment. In addition, rubrics encourage teachers to reflect on the validity and value of assignments not only before they are assigned but also after they are completed. This dual reflection time strengthens the assignment, the curriculum, and the assessment procedures, and aids in establishing a more rigorous curriculum.

Rubrics are also important to students. They provide students valuable information and take the mystery out of how an assignment is graded. By clearly defining what is needed for attaining particular levels of performance, rubrics answer students' age-old questions: "What does the teacher want?" "What do I have to do to get an 'A'?" Rubrics can also give students the kind of direction that enables them to approach projects with confidence. Rubrics guide students to set goals as they approach their tasks. When students set these goals, they are becoming more responsible for their learning. We all know that this empowerment raises students' confidence, and that confident students perform at a much higher level. We must keep in mind that it is not the "A" that enhances a student's self-esteem; it is the student with a high self-esteem that gets the "A."

There are many types of rubrics. Some rubrics are designed to assess work for specific subjects or one particular assignment, such as a special research project. These are generally referred to as subject-specific and task-specific rubrics. Other rubrics are more generic and can be used in a variety of situations. Still other rubrics are used to assess student attitudes and behavior, such as how well students work in a cooperative group, how well they listen as a member of an audience, and how prepared they are when they come to class.

Rubrics can be either holistic or analytical. A holistic rubric is used to assess a product in its totality and to determine, overall, what level of performance is shown. Analytical rubrics, on the other hand, target specific skills, such as organization, applying the scientific method, or using vivid verbs and concrete nouns in writing.

Rubrics, like so many other things in life, are often easier to understand by example rather than explanation, and that's why this section offers numerous examples of various types of rubrics. The first one, on the next page, is a rubric that can be used to assess employee work performance. Let's just hope it never is.

A Super Rubric
for Assessing Work Performance

	Awesome	Admirable	Acceptable	Amateur
Quality of Work	Leaps tall buildings in a single bound	Jumps over medium buildings with a running start	Uses a ladder to climb over buildings	Trips when stepping up to curbs
Productivity	Is faster than a speeding bullet	Is as fast as a speeding bullet if there's a good tailwind	Can arrive at the same time as the bullet if given a head start	Can beat a water pistol nine times out of ten
Ability to Take on Responsibility	More powerful than a locomotive	More powerful than a bus	Can push a stalled car	Needs a jump start
Ability to Perceive Needs	Can see through walls	Can see through wallpaper	Can peek over the top of walls	Can see through a window if the shades are up
Flexibility	Can bend steel with bare hands	Can bend lead with bare hands	Can bend aluminum foil with bare hands	Can break pencils if wearing protective gloves

LEVELS OF PERFORMANCE

The rubric on page 41 illustrates the differences in levels of performance specified on rubrics. As you look over this rubric, pay particular attention to the highlighted words. Notice how they differentiate one level from the next.

Because this is a six-level rubric, the difference from one level of performance to the next is rather narrow. If this were a three-level rubric, it would include only numbers 6, 4, and 1, and the differences would be much greater between the levels. It is often asked: "How many levels should there be?" The nature of the work being assessed will determine the number of levels needed, and you will see examples of six-, five-, four-, and three-level rubrics throughout this section.

I suggest that as you begin working with rubrics, you work with three-level rubrics. This way you can focus on high, medium, and low. After using a three-level rubric, you will find that it is easier to expand to a five- or six-level rubric. You may find when evaluating a product, that it is just a little better than a 3, so you give it a 3+. As you raise the 2 to a 2+ and the 1 to a 1+, you have created a six-level rubric.

Many teachers like to create five-level rubrics in which the third level is considered the middle ground, the "average" level. The other levels are then created from that basic description. One drawback of a five-level rubric is that the levels will be equated with the traditional grades of A, B, C, D, and F. Rubrics should lead students and parents away from letter grade evaluation to assessing levels of performance based upon specific areas and qualities. Rubrics should be seen as providing the information needed to raise students' levels of performance. Students can see specifically what needs to be done to improve. They usually respond to moving from one level to the next with, "I can do that."

Quality of Performance
for a Six-Level Rubric

6 This level of performance is the truly **exceptional**; everything about the project is **impressive**; the student has **exceeded** the requirements of the assignment; the required skills displayed are superior; it is apparent that the student has spent an **extraordinary** amount of time to complete the work.

5 This level of performance is **strong**; the work is **above-average**; the project **exceeds to some extent** the requirements of the assignment; the required skills displayed are **commendable; care and effort** are shown in the completion of the work.

4 This level of performance is **average**; the project **meets** all the requirements of the assignment but **does not extend beyond**; the required skills displayed are **adequate, reasonable care and effort** are shown.

3 This level of performance is **below average; deficiencies** in the project exist; the assignment is **incomplete**; the required skills displayed are **inadequate**; the project **lacks care and effort**.

2 This level of performance is **unacceptable**; important requirements for the project are **missing or unfinished**; the work is **careless; little evidence** of the required skills can be found; the project is **poorly done**.

1 This level of performance is **deficient; none** of the requirements for the project are complete; the work shows **no care; no evidence** of the required skills can be found; the project is **undone**.

GENERIC RUBRICS

Having looked at the distinctions between the various levels of performance, let us now examine how the levels of performance might be described in a rubric. On page 43, you'll see a generic rubric. It is so general that it can be used to assess a variety of types of student work. It also provides a solid start from which a more specific rubric can be developed. Note that each descriptor begins with a verb. Also note the parallel format of the descriptions.

A Generic Rubric

6
- Demonstrates conceptual understanding
- Is complete and goes beyond what is expected
- Presents clear rationale
- Presents specific, relevant details as evidence
- Represents exemplary achievement

5
- Demonstrates understanding
- Is complete
- Presents rationale
- Presents supporting evidence
- Represents commendable achievement

4
- Demonstrates some understanding
- Is fairly complete
- Presents a somewhat flawed rationale
- Presents supporting evidence that lacks detail
- Represents adequate achievement

3
- Attempts to show understanding but is unclear
- Is incomplete
- Presents a flawed rationale
- Lacks supporting details
- Represents some evidence of achievement

2
- Demonstrates obvious misconceptions
- Is sorely incomplete
- Presents no evidence or rationale
- Presents no examples
- Represents limited evidence of achievement

1
- Demonstrates no understanding
- Shows no real attempt
- Presents a restatement of the question
- Represents no evidence of achievement

THE LANGUAGE OF RUBRICS: PERFORMANCE DESCRIPTORS

The language of rubrics is important. The descriptions need to be specific and in sufficient detail so that students can use the rubric as a guide when completing assignments, and parents and students can see clearly how assignments are evaluated. As you saw in the rubric on the previous page, the descriptions from one level to the next need to correlate with each other. If a particular characteristic is mentioned in one level, it is included in all levels.

The chart on page 45 lists a variety of performance descriptors. Some rubrics simply use numbers to label the different performance levels, but others use performance descriptors, such as "awesome" and "amateur." There's no limit to the number of possible performance descriptors, and as you work with rubrics you may think of some especially appropriate descriptors for the kind of work you assess. You can even have students help develop and choose performance descriptors. Be sure to use descriptors consistently so that students develop an understanding of what the descriptors represent.

A Variety of Performance Descriptors

DESCRIPTORS FOR SIX-LEVEL RUBRICS

6   Exceptional: exemplary achievement

5   Strong: commendable achievement

4   Capable: adequate achievement

3   Developing: some evidence of achievement

2   Limited: limited evidence of achievement

1   Emergent: minimal evidence of achievement

DESCRIPTORS FOR FIVE-LEVEL RUBRICS

5   Impressive: outstanding

4   Notable: very effective

3   Adequate: effective

2   Minimal: marginally effective

1   Incomplete: ineffective

DESCRIPTORS FOR FOUR-LEVEL RUBRICS

4   Awesome: complete understanding

3   Admirable: adequate understanding

2   Acceptable: limited understanding

1   Amateur: little or no understanding

DESCRIPTORS FOR THREE-LEVEL RUBRICS

3   Strong: high achievement

2   Capable: adequate achievement

1   Developing: limited achievement

THE LANGUAGE OF RUBRICS: AREAS TO BE EVALUATED

Many rubrics list specific areas, or factors, that will be assessed such as "communication skills" and "organization." These headings describe the kind of skills, knowledge, and work habits that are demanded by the curriculum. They may be general enough to fit every possible assignment or so specific that they are meant only for one special task.

The chart on page 47 lists areas to be evaluated for four different potential rubrics. The rubrics are semi-generic, in other words, they could be used for many different assignments of one specific type. For example, the chart lists areas to be evaluated for any art project.

Remember that not all rubrics indicate specific factors or areas. Some, such as the generic rubric on page 43 and the rubric for listening skills on page 53, are used to assess work holistically rather than to target specific areas.

Areas to Be Evaluated in Semi-Generic Rubrics

FOR ANY SUBJECT OR PRODUCT

Content Knowledge
Critical Thinking Skills
Communication Skills

FOR AN ART PROJECT

Produces Quality Work
Uses Time Effectively
Accepts Responsibility
Communicates Effectively

FOR A WRITTEN PRODUCT

Organization
Content Accuracy
Research
Creativity
Presentation
Mechanics

FOR MATH OR SCIENCE ASSIGNMENTS

Conceptual Understanding: demonstrates in-depth understanding of the concepts, processes, principles, and skills

Processes and Strategies: selects effective procedures/strategies; presents work logically and coherently

Interprets Results: uses inferences/interpretations to answer the question posed and verify the solution

Communication: communicates thinking process effectively and clearly

RUBRICS FOR PROJECT WORK

The rubric on page 49 is an example of how the vocabulary we talked about on pages 44-47 can be used in a rubric. It includes levels of performance expressed in words (rather than numbers) running horizontally across the page. It also lists four areas to be evaluated running vertically down the page.

This rubric is a particularly useful rubric. It can be used to assess products that students have completed in groups. It evaluates both the final product (organization, content, presentation) and the process (cooperation).

A Rubric for Project Work

	Awesome	Admirable	Acceptable	Amateur
Organization	• Well organized • Logical format • Transitions from idea to idea were excellent, enhancing the project	• Thoughtfully organized • Easy to follow most of the time • Transitions easy to follow, but at times ideas unclear	• Somewhat organized • Somewhat incoherent • Transitions not always smooth and at times distracted the audience	• Choppy and confusing • Difficult to follow • Transitions were abrupt and distracted audience
Cooperation	• Worked extremely well with others • Solicited, respected, and complemented each other's ideas • Highly productive	• Worked very well with others • Worked to get everyone involved • Productive team	• Attempted to work well with others • At times "off task" and not everyone was actively involved	• Was dysfunctional • Did not respect each other's opinions • Argued often • Little or no teamwork
Content	• Excellent job of research • Utilized information effectively	• Good job of research • Utilized information in an efficient manner	• Acceptable job of research • Limited information	• Unacceptable job of research • Little or no fact gathering
Presentation	• Original, unique approach • Engaging, provocative	• Clever, at times unique • Well done, interesting	• Few original touches • At times interesting	• Predictable, bland • Did not keep audience interested

RUBRICS FOR GROUP WORK

Education is not only about acquiring, applying, and synthesizing knowledge, but also about developing positive attitudes and work habits. In March 1992, the U.S. Department of Labor published a report from the Secretary's Commission on Achieving Necessary Skills (SCANS). The report identified skills and competencies needed to produce a work force ready for the next century. It describes five competencies needed to ensure effective job performance.

1. Resources: student can identify, organize, plan, and allocate resources.

2. Interpersonal: student can work with others, lead, negotiate, and communicate.

3. Information: student can acquire, organize, interpret, and use information.

4. Systems: student can understand, monitor, and improve complex systems.

5. Technology: student can select, apply, and maintain a variety of technologies.

It is interesting to note that the Labor Department has pointed to the importance of developing positive attitudes and working and communicating with others. These interpersonal, or attitudinal, skills should be taught in our schools. Many of us use cooperative learning techniques in our classrooms. However, do we assess how well our students work cooperatively? Can we identify areas of strength and areas that need improvement?

The rubric on the next page can be used by students to self-assess how cooperatively their groups work. The rubric is presented in a very simple form, as a rating guide.

Measure Your Success

On a scale of 1 to 4 rank your group's success in working together.

1= poor   2= acceptable   3= good   4= best

1. Setting achievable goals   1 2 3 4

2. Organizing to work together to meet goals   1 2 3 4

3. Defining group roles   1 2 3 4

4. Accepting individual responsibility   1 2 3 4

5. Listening to each other with respect   1 2 3 4

6. Taking turns to speak   1 2 3 4

7. Using respectful voices   1 2 3 4

8. Encouraging one another   1 2 3 4

9. Eliminating put-downs   1 2 3 4

10. Requesting teacher help only when needed   1 2 3 4

11. Maintaining group order   1 2 3 4

12. Reaching our goals   1 2 3 4

Summary statement: Generally, I think our group...

_____

_____

_____

Name _____

SPECIFIC RUBRICS

Most of the rubrics you've seen in the preceding pages are generic. They can be used for a variety of subjects, products, and assignments. The next pages, 53-72, give examples of rubrics that are more specific, either to a particular subject, such as the rubric for writing on page 55, or to a specific task or assignment, such as the rubric for *The Pearl* on page 58. In many cases, the student assignment sheet appears along with the rubric so that you can see how the assignment and the assessment correlate.

The first specific rubric assesses a skill that teachers in every school in the land value—listening. How wonderful it would be if our students displayed good listening habits. One step toward that goal could be to hand out the rubric on the next page at the beginning of the school year and ask students to assess their listening skills. After this assessment, students should set some listening goals. Perhaps, then, students will come closer to the listening habits we want to see in our classrooms.

A Rubric for Listening Skills

Strong Listener

- Immediately responds to oral directions
- Focuses on speaker
- Sustains attention span
- Listens to others

Capable Listener

- Follows oral directions
- Usually attentive to speaker and discussion
- Listens to others without interrupting

Developing Listener

- Has difficulty following oral directions
- Relies on repetition
- Often inattentive
- Short attention span
- Often interrupts

LANGUAGE ARTS WRITING RUBRIC

The Language Arts rubric on the following page can be used for any piece of writing. It can be used as it is or you can select three or four areas (ideas, organization, voice, vocabulary) to be assessed. Some teachers have started using this rubric by concentrating on two areas and with each subsequent piece of writing adding a third area. It is important that students have copies of this rubric in their binders. The rubric provides a guideline as to what is exceptional writing, strong writing, and so on. This rubric is also an effective way to communicate expectations to parents.

A Rubric for Writing

Exceptional Writing

- Insightful and fully developed ideas
- Clear sentence sense; variety and transitions
- Superior vocabulary

Strong Writing

- Communicates insightful ideas
- Clear sentence sense; variety and transitions
- Strong vocabulary

Capable Writing

- Attempts to use insightful ideas
- Some sentence variety; few fragments and run-ons
- Grade level vocabulary

Developing Writing

- Attempts to communicate ideas
- Many simple sentences, fragments, and run-ons
- Ordinary vocabulary

Emerging Writing

- Limited development of ideas
- Simple sentences; many fragments and run-ons
- Ineffective vocabulary

Limited Writing

- Undeveloped ideas
- Unclear sentence structure
- Ineffective vocabulary

HELPFUL DEFINITIONS

Insightful: Ability to see deeply and sympathetically.

Transitions: Words that connect one idea to another, for example, *although, however, consequently.*

RUBRIC FOR A PERFORMANCE

The assignment on the next page was given to students after they finished reading *The Pearl,* by John Steinbeck. The students were asked to write a song related to the book and then perform it. They were enthusiastic and interested. But, they did have the age-old question: "How are you going to grade this?" What a good question. How *was* I going to grade this assignment? I decided to create a simple rubric. Note that the rubric used to assess this product is a three-level rubric. I felt that this type of creative, artistic assignment should not be dissected too finely. The students should be rewarded for the energy and effort they put forth to complete this work. Like pieces of art, the assessment of this product is quite subjective. The three-level rubric helps to add some objectivity.

The Pearl

PURPOSE: To write a song for *The Pearl*

PRODUCT: Performance of song—live, on audiotape, or as a music video

PROCEDURE: John Steinbeck writes in *The Pearl* that the making of songs was a rich tradition for Kino and his people: "His people had once been great makers of songs so that everything they saw or thought or did or heard became a song." (page 21) Throughout the novel five songs course through Kino's head. Three of these songs are: "Song of the Family," "Song of Evil," "Song of the Enemy." In your groups, you will write the lyrics for one of these songs. If you carefully follow these steps, you will be successful in your task.

1. Select one of the "songs" that interests you.

2. List some songs (country, rock, folk, etc.) that you might use as the basis for your "song."

3. Carefully reread those sections in which your selected song occurs. You can do this by dividing the book among the group members.

4. Copy some of the words from the text you think you might use in your lyrics.

5. Within your group discuss the meaning you want your song to have.

6. Use the words you have copied, your own words, thoughts from your discussions, and the insights you have gained from your journal writing and our class discussions to write the lyrics for your song.

You will be presenting your song to the class, and you can do this in one of three ways: as a live "concert," an audiotape, or a music video. Performances will be held on _____.

Rubric for *The Pearl*

3
- Lyrics demonstrate complete understanding of the plot.
- Meaning of the song is clear.
- Language is descriptive and interesting.
- Presentation has a "professional" look.
  - cover for videotape or audiotape
  - props for live "concert"
- Presentation is easily heard and understood.

2
- Lyrics demonstrate some understanding of plot.
- Meaning of song is somewhat clear.
- Language is interesting.
- Presentation is complete.
  - cover for videotape or audiotape
  - props for live "concert"
- Presentation is somewhat difficult to hear and understand.

1
- Lyrics are few and do not show understanding of the plot.
- Meaning of song is unclear.
- Language is repetitious and uninteresting.
- Presentation is lacking.
  - no cover for videotape or audiotape
  - no props for live "concert"
- Presentation is difficult to hear.

MATH PROBLEMS

On the following four pages, you'll find two different math problems and two different rubrics. It is interesting to compare the two rubrics. The first rubric was used once a week for weekly open-ended math problems, such as the one on page 60. Called the "Problem of the Week," or POW for short, these weekly problems were introduced every Monday and turned in on Fridays. Students were encouraged to use diagrams and charts and to write thorough explanations of how they arrived at their solutions.

The second rubric, on page 63, was developed specifically for the second math problem, on page 62. The second rubric is very similar to the first rubric, but it includes details about fractions. The second rubric shows how easily a more general rubric can be adapted into an assignment-specific rubric. Also, the text is written in paragraphs rather than bulleted lists. Teachers should feel free to write and adapt rubrics to meet their specific writing styles and assessment needs.

Math Problem of the Week:
A Strange Tug-of-War

PURPOSE: To solve a math problem

PRODUCT: Solution explained in words, numbers, and diagrams

PROCEDURE: Read the problem below. Think about it by yourself, with your friends, and/or with your family. Use words, numbers, and diagrams to record your solution and turn it in Friday morning.

In the San Mateo County Fair Tug-of-War competition, the computer found that three teams were equally matched, and they are described below.

In the first round of competition, four middle school students competed as a team utilizing their equally well developed strength. On the other side of the rope were five math teachers who had practiced together for many, many years. Each of the teachers had the same amount of strength. When these two teams competed, the result was a tie.

In the second round one team was made up of Rowdy, a specially trained tugging dog. Rowdy was pitted against a team made up of two math teachers and one middle school student. Again the contest was a tie.

The final match was between Rowdy and three of the math teachers on one side and four of the middle school students on the other side. Who will win this final match?

WORK SPACE

Source: Donna Morris, Math Teacher, Burlingame Intermediate School

Math Problem of the Week Rubric

4
- Fully accomplishes the purpose of the task
- Shows full grasp and use of the central mathematic ideas in the problem
- Communicates the solution clearly and accurately using some combination of written, symbolic, or visual means (charts, graphs, lists)

3
- Substantially accomplishes the purpose of the task
- Shows an essential grasp of the central mathematic ideas in the problem
- Communicates the solution to the problem

2
- Partially accomplishes the purpose of the task
- Shows partial but limited grasp of the central mathematic ideas of the problem
- Does not communicate the solution to the problem clearly, completely, or accurately

1
- Shows little or no progress toward accomplishing the purpose of the task
- Shows little or no grasp of the central mathematic ideas of the problem
- Barely (if at all) communicates a solution to the problem

0
- Did not attempt the problem
- Did not turn in the problem

Source: Donna Morris, Math Teacher, Burlingame Intermediate School

Performance-Based Math Task

PURPOSE: To solve a problem using fractions

PRODUCT: Solution and diagram written below

PROCEDURE: Read and solve the following problem. Use the space below to illustrate and explain your solution. Your answer must have:

- diagrams
- labels for diagrams
- appropriate math vocabulary
- written explanation of your thinking
- clear statement of results
- all possibilities

For my birthday, I received a wonderful cake! The cake had three different flavors—chocolate, carrot, and lemon. The cake was divided into twelfths. Four-twelfths of the cake was chocolate. The rest of the cake was carrot and lemon. There was a different amount of each cake flavor.

How many combinations of twelfths could the carrot and lemon cake represent?

WORK SPACE

Rubric for Scoring
Performance-Based Math Task

4 A clear diagram must reflect an understanding of fractions. The explanation must use appropriate math vocabulary and include the correct answer. The written explanation must include strategies and observations and there should be a clear statement of the result.

3 The answer must include the correct solution but may not be as complete as a "4" response. The drawing is less precise, the language is less well-developed, and the sequence may not be evident.

2 The answer may have an incorrect solution or an incorrect number of solutions. Some organization is shown. The diagram is unclear, and the writing is adequate.

1 The work shows only a partial attempt. There is no solution or an incorrect solution. Diagram is missing or incomplete.

Source: Burlingame School District, Burlingame, CA

SCIENCE PROJECT

The following science project served as a fun and creative way for students to review what they had learned about invertebrates. The student assignment sheet is given on pages 65-66, and the rubric used to assess the assignment follows on page 67. This rubric has a slightly different look and style from many of the other rubrics in this book. It's presented more in the form of a rating guide. It's important to keep in mind that rubrics can have many different styles and appearances. What is common to all rubrics is that they serve as systematic guides for assessing student work. Given those broad parameters, teachers should feel comfortable adapting rubrics in any way that best fits their needs. This particular rubric (and the one on page 72 as well) was used by students to assess their own and their peers' work. To help students use the rubric effectively, the science teacher led a class discussion about how the various levels actually looked. Students were then armed with the same basic understanding, which allowed for a more consistent evaluation process.

Invertebrate Newspaper Project

PURPOSE: To share and review the information you have learned about the invertebrates you've studied

PRODUCT: An invertebrate newspaper

PROCEDURE: In your group of eight experts (one expert representing each of the eight different phyla or groups of invertebrates), you will create a newspaper with articles describing and explaining your invertebrates. Your group should decide if the newspaper will be written from the point of view of a human being or of an invertebrate. Each expert must write an article about her/his invertebrate. The article should include the information listed below:

ARTICLE CONTENTS

1. Classification:

> Common name
> Phylum name
> Scientific name (if you have it)
> Classes or sub-groups in your phylum

2. Environment and adaptation(s) for that environment

3. How your invertebrate is viewed by people

4. Body Plan:

> Symmetry
> Segmented body
> Appendages
> Body covering

5. Movement:

> How does your invertebrate move?
> When does your invertebrate move and why?
> Adaptation(s) for movement

6. Reproduction:

> Life Cycle
> How does your invertebrate reproduce?
> How does your invertebrate change during its Life Cycle?
> Adaptation(s) for growth and reproduction

NEWSPAPER ARTICLES/SECTIONS:

Your newspaper should include articles for at least eight of the following sections:

Human Interest	Interviews
Entertainment	Crossword Puzzle
Television	Business and Career
Sports	Editorials
Classified	Advice
Life Styles	Weather
Comics	Announcements (marriages, births, deaths)
Movies	Personals

TIMELINE:

Monday:	article rough draft due for self- and peer-evaluation
Tuesday:	revised final article due
Wednesday:	newspaper due for original group- and peer group-evaluation
Thursday:	review for invertebrate cooperative test using newspapers
Friday:	invertebrate cooperative test

Source: Lily Ning, Science Teacher, Burlingame Intermediate School

Invertebrate Newspaper Evaluation

Name_____ Date_____

Your Newspaper Group_____

Rate your newspaper and the newspapers of two other groups.

1 = poor
2 = barely passable
3 = average
4 = good
5 = excellent

EVALUATION CATEGORIES:

	YOURS	OTHER 1	OTHER 2
1. Presentation			
Title Page	_____	_____	_____
Layout	_____	_____	_____
Overall	_____	_____	_____
2. Content			
Is there a variety of article types?	_____	_____	_____
Is the newspaper informative on all the various invertebrates?	_____	_____	_____
Are all the phyla represented?	_____	_____	_____

3. List three things that make your newspaper interesting and unique.

_____

_____

4. List three reasons why people should read your newspaper.

_____

_____

Source: Lily Ning, Science Teacher, Burlingame Intermediate School

RUBRIC FOR AN ORAL PRESENTATION

The speech assignment on the next page was given after students had completed a thematic language arts unit on prejudice. The students had given speeches prior to this activity and therefore had received instructions on how to deliver a speech. Students evaluated each others' presentations using the rating guide on pages 70 and 71. The rubric on page 72 gives specific details about each performance level so that students would have a solid and consistent understanding of what their ratings meant. It is important for students who are self- or peer-evaluating to have a very clear sense of each level. While these levels are often discussed in class directly before students use rating guides, it is more effective to actually write out the levels in rubric form so that students can refer to them throughout and after the evaluation process.

Newspaper Presentation

PURPOSE: To give an oral presentation about prejudice

PRODUCT: Newspaper presentation

PROCEDURE: The newspaper informs us about the events and activities that go on in our daily lives. While many of us might read the newspaper, we don't always discuss everything we have read. Think of all the issues that fill the newspaper daily. Think of all the stimulating and interesting conversations we could have just talking about the different ideas in the newspaper. Because of all the information we can find in the newspaper, we will use it as the basis for our speeches.

Each group of three students will be required to read one newspaper article which relates to the theme we've been studying — prejudice. Every group will prepare a presentation about the article they selected. Each member must speak. The presentation should include three parts, and each group member will present one of these parts:

1. **Summary:** give a brief summary of the article, including the who, what, where, when, and how.

2. **Causes:** explain why you think this happened.

3. **Solutions:** suggest at least one detailed idea about how your group would make sure this doesn't happen again.

Be sure you prepare thoroughly. Use note cards to keep on track. We are all interested in what you have to say, so please speak loudly and clearly during your presentation.

Newspaper Presentation Evaluation Form

Name of article: _____

Speaker #1: _____

Summary: How well did the speaker summarize the article? Were the questions of who, what, where, when, and how answered? Was the information presented clearly? Circle a rating for this speaker (4 is best).

1   2   3   4

Give specific reasons for your rating.

_____

_____

_____

_____

Speaker #2: _____

Causes: Does the speaker clearly state what might have been the cause of this particular situation? Does she/he give specific details? Circle a rating for this speaker.

1   2   3   4

Give specific reasons for your rating.

_____

_____

_____

_____

Speaker #3: _____

Solutions: Does the speaker offer specific detailed solutions for this situation? Are they reasonable? Are they stated clearly? Circle a rating for this speaker.

1   2   3   4

Give specific reasons for your rating.

_____
_____
_____
_____

Presentation as a Whole

How well do you think the group did as a whole? How effective, interesting, and informative was the presentation? Circle a rating for this presentation. Follow the lead of the man in the chair!

1   2   3   4

Give specific reasons for your rating.

_____
_____
_____
_____
_____
_____
_____
_____

Newspaper Presentation Rubric

4
- Communicates understanding
- Presents clear rationale
- Presents specific, relevant details as evidence
- Goes beyond what is expected
- Maintains eye contact
- Has none or relatively few vocal fillers
- Can be heard

3
- Demonstrates some understanding
- Is somewhat complete
- Presents a rationale
- Has some supporting details
- Maintains some eye contact
- Has relatively few vocal fillers
- Can be heard

2
- Attempts to show understanding but is unclear
- Presents minimum evidence, which is flawed
- Is lacking in supporting details
- Presents inappropriate examples
- Does not maintain good eye contact (reads from paper)
- Has many vocal fillers
- Is difficult to hear

1
- Demonstrates obvious misconceptions
- Presents no rationale or evidence
- Demonstrates no real understanding
- Presents no examples
- Does not make eye contact (reads from paper)
- Has many vocal fillers
- Cannot be heard

CREATING RUBRICS

Now that we have looked at a number of rubrics, it is time to examine how to go about creating a rubric. Keep in mind that developing a rubric is a systematic task. As is often the case, you will find that the more you practice, the easier it will be to write your own rubrics. In fact, you will be able to teach your students how to create rubrics. (When students are involved in developing their own rubrics, their performance level usually goes up.) Here are some general guidelines to use when writing rubrics:

- A rubric must include specific descriptions that spell out each level of achievement.
- The descriptions need to be listed in parallel fashion.
- Writing should begin with the highest level of achievement and completed in descending order from exemplary achievement to no achievement.
- The descriptions must be written in positive terms.

How do you determine the number of levels in your rubric? Is a six-level rubric better than a five-level one? The assignment being assessed and your experience with rubrics will help to determine the number of levels to use. If rubrics are new to you, start simply with a three-level rubric, such as the rubric for listening skills on page 53. You can also try developing the kind of rubric proposed by the state of Oregon: an open-ended six-level rubric. Levels 5, 3, and 1 are described in detail, and levels 6, 4, and 2 are left blank. This format allows an evaluator to move up or down based upon the piece of work being assessed. For example, if a project is just a little better than a 5, or a 5+, it can be given a 6.

The next step is to determine which areas will be evaluated, such as organization, content, procedures, process, and mechanics. There is no magic number of areas that should be evaluated. This is determined by the nature and purpose of the assignment.

The decisions you make about the type of rubric you're designing are really based on your instructional goals, which in turn are dependent on district or state standards. You need to think about not only what you want students to learn but also how you will know that they have learned it and, more importantly, to what degree they have learned it.

In general, a rubric should be designed before you give an assignment so that students can look at the rubric and set goals for the level they would like to achieve. There are times, however, when you will design a rubric after students have completed the assignment. There are also times when you will need to revise a rubric after using it. In either case, here are some general steps to follow:

- Look at real student work.
- Sort the work into broad levels of achievement: high, medium, and low.
- Find strong examples for each level.
- Start with the most perfect response to the assignment. If none can be found, imagine what one would look like.
- Decide what characterizes each level of performance.
- Write these characteristics into a rubric.
- Describe each level of performance in a positive manner.

The Exemplary Chocolate Chip Cookie

Do you think you are ready to try your hand at developing a rubric? Why not start with something fun and familiar—a chocolate chip cookie. I've assigned this seemingly easy task to groups of teachers in assessment workshops. The participants realized, after much lively discussion and laughter, that creating group rubrics takes time, good listening skills, and compromise. Gather together a group of your colleagues and try writing a rubric for a chocolate chip cookie using the blank form on page 75. Be sure you include performance descriptors as well as areas to be evaluated. After you have written your own rubric, take a look at the one on page 76, which was written by teachers in Castroville, Texas.

Your Rubric for
Chocolate Chip Cookies

Another Rubric
for Chocolate Chip Cookies

	Awesome	Adequate	Awful
Chippage	A little dough with your chips?	A chocolate chip with every bite.	Couldn't find a chip with a magnifying glass.
Taste	Melts in your mouth.	Almost home-made.	Tastes like a handful of sawdust.
Size	TEXAS size!	Comfortably fits in your hand.	One calorie per serving.
Chewability	Perfect late night snack.	Milk may be necessary.	You could shingle a roof with it.

Source: Bridget Bauml, Timothy Boland, Jennilea Campbell, DoraJean Clark, and Katherine Poska, Elective Teachers, Medina Valley Junior High School.

Establishing a Portfolio Program

PART 3

PURPOSES OF PORTFOLIOS

A portfolio is a systematic collection of student work chosen by the student and teacher to show progress in one or more content areas. It is more than a file folder filled with student work. It is more than a notebook compiled at the end of a unit of study. A portfolio is a collection of work over time that reflects processes, products, achievement, and progress. It is valuable to the teacher, the student, and to the student's family/guardian.

Portfolios have many purposes. Individual classrooms and entire schools need to give serious thought to the role portfolios should play in their assessment programs. In thinking through what purposes portfolios will have in your classroom and in your school, it can be helpful to look at the benefits of using portfolios.

Few other traditional assessment practices of the past or present have afforded students the opportunity to assume such an integral part in their own learning. Students set personal goals as they create their portfolios. The student work found within portfolios reflects the accomplishment of these goals. Because students are encouraged to include examples of how they arrived at their goals, they are able to see their own progress over time. Students feel a pride of ownership for their work, and they see the personal and academic relevance of the work they have completed. Most importantly, students value themselves as learners as they proceed through the portfolio process of selecting work and reflecting upon each piece. They are able to see their accomplishments. This assessment process emphasizes what students can do, not what they cannot do. This positive approach enables students to reach higher levels of accomplishment.

In summary, portfolios help students to:
- determine meaningful work
- reflect on their strengths and needs
- set learning goals
- see their own progress over time
- think about ideas presented in their work
- see the effort they put forth

- feel ownership and pride in their work
- realize their work has personal relevance.

Another major purpose for portfolios is to assist teachers in curriculum and instruction decisions. By reviewing the work students have accomplished, teachers can adjust or modify the curricular and instructional programs as needed. Curriculum and instruction can be validated, improved, or even extended based upon information gained from a critical look at class-room portfolios.

Portfolios are also useful to teachers because they provide a vehicle for collecting work that exemplifies process. In other words, portfolios provide opportunities to assess not just end products but how students arrived at their end products. The chart on page 81 shows the learning processes that are involved in various student products.

When portfolios play this role of showing students' processes for learning, they can be used as a diagnostic tool for the class as a whole as well as for individual students. Because of this process orientation, teachers can become more aware of students' learning styles and thereby plan activities and instructional strategies accordingly. In addition, based on the ideas and thinking revealed in the portfolios, teachers are able to evaluate individual student needs. Teachers can become aware of student learning difficulties and uncover problems needing attention in many areas, such as skill development, written expression, collaboration with others, and growth in ability level. In addition, portfolios provide another means for dialogue between students and teacher so that teachers can better support students' needs in both the affective and cognitive realms.

Parents, guardians, and family members assume a key role in the portfolio process as they review, respond, and recognize the work of students. Although family involvement is an optional role in a portfolio program, many families relish the opportunity. They can provide the recognition students need, which helps to foster student self-esteem. Bringing together students and family members to review portfolios provides the family-school connection, and this connection is vital to student success. Parents are curious about their children's progress, and portfolios allow them the opportunity to see progress over time.

Examples of Learning Processes
Shown by Specific Products

PROCESS: *WHAT* STUDENTS DO TO LEARN	PRODUCT: THE RESULT OR END-PRODUCT
Clusters, Webs, Maps, Brainstorms, Lists	Essay, Published Book, Skit, Report, HyperCard® Stacks
Learning Log Pages	History Report, Science Report, Newspaper Project
Literature Journal	List of Books Read, Book Talk, Book Commercial
Journal Pages	Polished Piece of Writing
Note Cards, Concept Cards, Outlines, Class Notes	Science Test, History Test
Graphic Organizers (Webs, Flowcharts, Cause and Effect Charts)	Retelling of Story or Historical Event, Cause and Effect Drawings
Reading or Recording of Poem or Song	Audiotape, Videotape
Journal of Experiments	Final Product for a Unit on Electricity

There are a variety of ways to invite family members to review their children's portfolios (and these are discussed in more detail on page 103):

- in a formal setting arranged by the teacher in the classroom
- at home with the aid of formatted response sheets
- during parent conferences in which the student leads the conference using the portfolio as the focal point
- at a "Back to School Night" when parents have a chance to look over the contents
- during a specially scheduled "Portfolio Presentation Night."

The chart on page 83 presents some of the major purposes of a portfolio program.

Purposes of Portfolios

PURPOSES	RESULTS
Monitoring Students' Progress	Promotes Growth
Evaluating Students' Achievement	Recognizes Students' Accomplishments
Making Instructional Decisions	Improves Instruction
Evaluating Programs	Modifies Programs

SETTING UP A PORTFOLIO PROGRAM

There are two key factors which must be considered when setting up a portfolio program as an assessment tool. One is the structure of the school, and the other is administrative requirements.

The structure of your school affects how you will use portfolios as well as how you will manage the logistics of collecting and storing them. You need to consider the following questions:

- Is your school organized by self-contained classrooms, single-subject classrooms, core (two subjects joined together and taught by one teacher), or interdisciplinary teams?
- Does your master schedule consist of single periods or block schedules?

Self-Contained Classrooms

If you teach in a self-contained classroom, you may want to begin using portfolios simply and focus only on one subject. Generally speaking, language arts lends itself best to portfolio assessment because it involves many open-ended questions and student products. In addition, there are many opportunities to show work in progress. Each student can collect all her/his assigned projects and papers in a working portfolio, or workfolio. Students can then choose favorite pieces from their workfolios to put into showcase portfolios. A student's showcase portfolio will be shared with an audience, such as peers and family members. In subsequent years you can incorporate other subject areas in the workfolios and showcase portfolios.

Single-Subject Classrooms

If your school is organized by single subjects or is departmentalized, you might create separate portfolios in designated subject areas, e.g., math, science, history. During the first year of portfolio assessment, you should move slowly and concentrate on developing and experiencing the process of portfolio assessment. Therefore, we suggest that you select your smallest and brightest class this first year. Once you have mastered the process, including the logistics and management, you can add your other classes. Finally, each student can create a showcase portfolio that is a compilation of meaningful work from all subject areas. In this process, students select pieces from their workfolios in each subject area and then compile them into showcase portfolios housed in one classroom such as the language arts classroom. The logistics for creating this showcase portfolio need to be coordinated among several teachers.

Interdisciplinary Teams

If you teach on an interdisciplinary team, you can devise a procedure within this team. The suggestions described above work well for a team configuration.

There are many different options for creating and coordinating a portfolio program based on your school organization. Review some of the possibilities below and determine what kind of portfolio program best suits your needs:

- a portfolio that targets one subject area within your classroom
- a showcase portfolio of all subject areas taught within your classroom
- several individual portfolios for each of the subject areas within your classroom or school
- a showcase portfolio of all subject areas within the school
- a showcase portfolio for your interdisciplinary team

When establishing a portfolio program, it is important to look at the school as a whole. The questions listed on the planning guide on page 86 need to be addressed by the staff in order to devise and implement an effective portfolio program. Professional readings need to be made available, staff development must be offered, and time must be provided for thorough discussions.

Planning Guide

1. What is your school organization?

   _____

2. What is your school's philosophy concerning portfolio assessment?

   _____

   _____

3. Does your school already have certain portfolio requirements, e.g., are portfolios used for parent conferences and/or to determine placement at the next level in a subject such as algebra?

   _____

   _____

4. What subjects would you like to include in students' portfolios?

   _____

   _____

5. How are students going to collect work from different subject areas or classrooms?

   _____

   _____

6. Will there be any guidelines for the kind of work that will be included in portfolios?

   _____

   _____

7. When will the work be chosen and the showcase portfolios presented? Are portfolio days designated on the school calendar?

   _____

   _____

8. Will the portfolio follow the student to the next grade, or will the student take the portfolio home? In other words, who owns the portfolio?

   _____

   _____

SELECTING THE CONTENTS OF THE PORTFOLIO

Because portfolios have a number of purposes, there are many types of work that can be included in them, such as: student writing (first drafts and polished pieces); individual and group products; investigations; diagrams, graphs, and charts; work written in the student's primary language; photographs of student work (items too bulky to fit); audiotapes, videotapes, and computer disks; and related assignments completed at different times.

Both students and teachers can be involved in the process of selecting the contents of portfolios, and there are a variety of approaches that can be used. Some teachers are loosely directive in what they expect. For example, they may direct students to include at least one sample of work from a specific unit (see pages 101-102 for more examples). Other teachers are explicitly directive and create a list of required items mentioning units of study, particular assignments, and specific skills. Students may have the option to include other samples of work; however, the teacher-required pieces must be included. In some classrooms, students have complete autonomy in selecting meaningful work, and teachers simply remind students after assignments are completed that if their work evokes pride, shows progress, or is meaningful, they may want to include the work in their portfolios.

It is important to keep in mind that portfolio assessment is not summative but formative; it is an ongoing process that starts at the beginning of the year and continues to the end of the year. Also, we must constantly remind ourselves and our students that portfolios include work that shows process not just final products.

The next four pages show how you can introduce both students and parents to portfolios and help them understand the contents and the on-going nature of the portfolio process. Pages 88 and 89 help students understand how to begin collecting work. Pages 90 and 91 are letters home that explain, at the beginning and end of the year, what portfolios are and how the family can be involved.

Portfolio Guidelines for Students

This year you will be creating a portfolio, a collection of the work you will have done throughout the year. Your portfolio will include work that is meaningful, that you like and are proud of, and that shows both progress and achievement. You will collect work in three subject areas:

1. _____

2. _____

3. _____

In each classroom, you will have a working portfolio (workfolio). You will collect all your assigned work in this workfolio. You will then choose specific pieces of work from this workfolio to create a showcase portfolio. (You will be using two types of portfolios—workfolios and showcase portfolios.)

When your showcase portfolio is complete, you will present it to:

_____

I will give you a checklist of all the types of items you will need to put in your showcase portfolio. We'll talk about how your portfolio will look and how you'll collect your work later. For now, I just want you to be aware of this project so you can begin thinking about what you will want to put in your showcase portfolio. Your showcase portfolio will include items such as:

- essays, research papers, narratives, poetry
- brainstorming sheets, planning sheets, clusters, outlines, webs, notes
- journals or journal pages, notebooks, learning logs
- graphs, charts

- drawings, collages, watercolors
- tests, quizzes, exams
- photographs of items too large to fit in your portfolio
- evidence of group projects: planning sheets, daily logs, notes
- audiotapes videotapes
- computer disks.

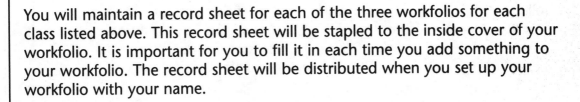

You will maintain a record sheet for each of the three workfolios for each class listed above. This record sheet will be stapled to the inside cover of your workfolio. It is important for you to fill it in each time you add something to your workfolio. The record sheet will be distributed when you set up your workfolio with your name.

How will you select your work? Any work you choose to include in your showcase portfolio should be something that you feel shows:

- thoughtful and insightful writing
- that you learned what was taught
- improvement
- effort
- achievement

Finally, you will write your thoughts about each piece of work you select and about your portfolio as a whole. I will give you specific directions about how to write these self-reflections later.

I know this sounds like a big project. It is! But it will also be very meaningful to you, because you will see your achievement and your progress over time. Class time will be provided for working on your port-folios, and I will be here to guide you through the process.

A Letter to Parents
at the Beginning of the Year

Dear Parents/Guardians:

During this school year, your daughter/son will be creating a portfolio, which is a collection of work completed throughout the year. It will include work that is meaningful, that shows both progress and achievement, and that your daughter/son is proud of and particularly likes. This work will be collected in three subject areas:

1. _____

2. _____

3. _____

Each student will not only collect the work but will also organize it for presentation in a showcase portfolio. In addition, each student will reflect on every piece of work in the portfolio as a means of self-evaluation. I hope that this system of collecting, organizing, and reflecting will help students look at how they learn, what they have learned, and how well they have learned. Our portfolio program is designed to show what students can do, rather than what they cannot do. It is a positive process of assessment.

If you have any questions, please call me.

Sincerely,

A Letter to Parents
at the End of the Portfolio Process

Dear Parents/Guardians:

As you know, the students have been working hard this year to put together portfolios of their work. I am happy to report that they have successfully completed this process. They selected work of which they are particularly proud. You will find that some of the pieces are completed efforts while others may be plans or work in progress. The important factor in the content of the portfolio is that these are the pieces of work that your daughter/son chose to share with you.

Please review this portfolio with your daughter/son and complete the comment sheet found in the portfolio on page ___.

Presenting a portfolio is a very important part of your student's learning experience. She/he is proud of what has been accomplished and would like to share it with you. This gives you an opportunity to see what your daughter/son can do. The positive feedback that you give is invaluable.

Thank you for your cooperation throughout this entire process and most importantly, thank you for your encouraging attitude.

Sincerely,

PORTFOLIO CONTENTS

While there are many ways to organize a portfolio, the following is a good model. It is summarized briefly in the chart on page 93.

Unifying Theme: Students should choose a unifying theme or style to tie their portfolio pages together. This can be done graphically by using a consistent border design or logo and/or verbally by using quotations. Provide students with time to think about this unifying theme.

Cover: Creating the cover and other pages of the portfolio takes time. Give each student a list of requirements for the cover, e.g., that it should incorporate the unifying theme, be attractive, and include specific information such as title, name, school year, and subjects.

To the Reader: Each student writes a letter, poem, or other piece of prose that serves as an invitation to read the portfolio as well as an explanation of the purpose and contents. Writing this piece gives students an opportunity to reflect on what they have accomplished and to celebrate the learning that has occurred.

Table of Contents: Students list the titles and page numbers of everything included, and this process enables students to check their organization. It should be completed at the end of the process.

Dividers: Dividers can be used to separate subjects or to identify categories such as completed work, work in progress, art work. Allow students flexibility in organizing their portfolios. The dividers can match the style of the cover and can help give portfolios a finished look.

Content Piece: The major ingredients in a showcase portfolio are the content pieces, the actual pieces of student work. Examples of the kind of content pieces that might be included in a portfolio can be found on pages 101–102.

Content Reflection, Reader Comment Page, and Teacher Comment Page: Descriptions and sample forms for these items can be found on pages 94-99.

Portfolio Contents

ITEM	EXPLANATION
Cover Page	Student creates a cover page complete with title, student name, and school year.
To the Reader	Student writes a letter to the reader introducing the portfolio.
Table of Contents	Student lists contents and corresponding page numbers.
Dividers	Student can include dividers at appropriate places throughout the portfolio.
Content Pieces	Student and/or teacher choose(s) pieces of student work.
Content Reflection	Student reflects on each content piece.
Reader Comment Page	This page invites comments and reflections from whomever reads the portfolio.
Teacher Comment Page	This page invites comments by the teacher.

CONTENT REFLECTION

A very important aspect of the portfolio process is the opportunity portfolios provide for student reflection. Students complete a content reflection page for each content piece that they include in their portfolios. The content reflection page may include any or all of the following:

- information about why the student chose to include this particular piece of work
- what the student might have learned about herself or himself and what was learned as a result of this effort.

Content reflection pages can lead the portfolio reader into insights about the student, and more importantly, students can draw insights about themselves. Be sure to give students time to reflect on their work as soon as possible after they have completed the work. A sample content reflection page is shown on the next page.

Content Reflection

1. Why did you select this piece of work? Give at least two or three reasons.

_____

_____

2. What do you see as the strengths of this piece of work? Give at least two or three reasons.

_____

_____

3. What was particularly important to you while you were completing this piece of work?

_____

_____

4. What things did you struggle with while you were doing this work?

_____

_____

5. If you could work more on this, what would you do?

_____

_____

6. What were some of the reactions you received from those who looked at this piece of work?

_____

_____

7. How is this piece of work the same as or different from other projects you have done?

_____

_____

READER COMMENT PAGE

The reader comment page is a sensitive area for a number of reasons. First, the reader must be guided through the comment process so that negative comments do not appear on the reader comment page. Letters home, comments to parents/guardians at "Back to School Nights," and articles in parent newsletters are all ways to communicate the important message that portfolio readers should not write negative remarks in portfolios.

Second, a student may have included some particularly sensitive material in the portfolio that she/he does not want to share with parents. To avoid this problem, encourage students to not include private, sensitive material in their showcase portfolios. If students insist, these materials can be removed before the reader begins reviewing the portfolio and then added back after the reader has finished.

Reader Comment Page

1. What is your initial reaction to reading this portfolio?

_____

_____

_____

_____

2. What changes have you noticed in this student's ability in any subject area?

_____

_____

_____

_____

3. What do this student's content reflections tell about her/him?

_____

_____

_____

_____

4. Which piece of work did you particularly like? Why?

_____

_____

_____

5. Is there any observation/thought you would like to share with this student?

_____

_____

_____

_____

TEACHER COMMENT PAGE

As teachers we, too, must be careful not to include negative remarks in students' portfolios. We need to model constructive criticism. Our comments can be in the form of questions to help students evaluate their efforts. One way to establish the kind of supportive tone needed for this page is for teachers to write their comments in the form of a personal letter to students. A possible format is included on the following page.

Teacher Comment Page

Dear _____:

Thank you for the opportunity to read through your portfolio. I like

_____

_____

_____

_____

_____

_____

_____

I particularly like

_____

_____

_____

_____

_____

_____

_____

_____

Thank you for sharing your portfolio with me.

Sincerely,

CHOOSING CONTENT PIECES

We now must turn our attention to the content pieces. Which pieces of student work should be included in a portfolio? On the following two pages you will find a checklist for students that suggests what might go into a portfolio. Your curriculum will determine what you should include on your list.

This student checklist can help students select their pieces and keep themselves organized. It becomes a great reference when it's time to develop the table of contents.

Portfolio Checklist:
Criteria for a Complete Portfolio

Name _____   Grade _____

My portfolio includes completion of work which is demonstrated by:

Title of assignment where this is shown:

Language Arts

- a major piece of writing
- improvement in writing
- a variety of writing types
- a variety of literature read
- interpretation of readings
- a long-range project that integrates skills
- a complete process of work including revision
- a piece of writing showing reflection

Social Studies

- an understanding of geography
- an understanding of current events
- an understanding of historical concepts
- connections between history and contemporary issues

Mathematics

- applications of math concepts in "real-life" situations

- an ability to solve problems

_____

- using math through charts, graphs, etc.

_____

Science

- use of data analysis

_____

- using measurements

_____

- using the scientific method

_____

- understanding scientific concepts

_____

Physical Education

- benefits of a healthy life style

_____

- an understanding of athletic activities

_____

Electives/Unified Arts

- creative/artistic expression

_____

- interpretation

_____

- use of multiple mediums including media, technology

_____

General

- a project involving research

_____

- an interdisciplinary unit

_____

- evidence of working cooperatively

_____

- contributions to the work of others

_____

- effective use of resources

_____

- use of technology

_____

- contributions to community

_____

- effective presentation to others

_____

- reflection and evaluation of own work

_____

SHARING PORTFOLIOS

Once the portfolio is complete, it needs an audience. There are a number of ways students can share their portfolios with family and friends. Here are a few ideas.

Portfolio Review at Home

Students take their portfolios home and present them to their parents or guardians. Be sure to attach a letter, such as the one on page 91, directing the reader to fill in the reader's comment page.

In-Class Portfolio Day

Students present their portfolios to each other during a special day scheduled just for this activity. Explain the day in advance and give students time to plan and rehearse what they will present. Because it can be somewhat cumbersome and uninteresting for everyone to listen to everyone's presentation, divide the students into groups of four. Students then take turns presenting their portfolios to the members of their groups. After these group presentations, students display their portfolios so that all classmates have the opportunity to see each others' work.

Portfolio Presentation Night

This special event can be scheduled in the evening or after school. Students create and send invitations to whomever they wish: parents, friends, siblings, or a former teacher. They then present their portfolios to their invited guests. Students are often very enthusiastic about presenting their portfolios to former kindergarten or primary grade teachers. It is a wonderful way to show those who got them started how far they have progressed.

Parent Conferences

Students can lead parent conferences using their portfolios as vehicles for discussion. This activity brings a positive atmosphere and focus to the conferences. Before the parent conferences actually occur, discuss with students the purpose and agenda of a conference and give each of them an opportunity to role-play a conference.

MANAGING A PORTFOLIO PROGRAM

The management system in portfolio assessment is vital. As discussed on page 84, the organization of your school determines the management system. Teachers in self-contained classrooms and on interdisciplinary teams can establish whatever system best fits into the classroom/team procedures. However, most middle school and high school teachers are responsible for many students throughout the day. Therefore, it is important to have a workfolio—showcase portfolio system. Workfolios are kept in each classroom and serve as places for students to keep work that may eventually go into showcase portfolios. The student is responsible for the workfolio in each subject area classroom. The teacher is responsible for encouraging students to select work and for providing time so that students can place items in their workfolios. The showcase portfolio is housed in one classroom.

Where to store all the portfolios is a major issue to consider, and there are many alternatives. Crates that contain hanging folders are perfect for housing portfolios. A manila folder can be stored in the hanging folder so that the hanging folders can be used each year. Using stackable containers saves classroom space. You can color code the crates and folders by housing all the workfolios in one color and all the showcase portfolios in another color.

Whatever storage and management system you select, students should have regular access to their workfolios. They should be encouraged to enter work at anytime. Be sure, however, to schedule several specific times for students to add to their workfolios and showcase portfolios. Sufficient time must be planned if the portfolio process is going to succeed.

The chart on the following page reviews the responsibilities and roles of both teachers and students in the portfolio process.

Teacher and Student Roles in the Portfolio Process

TEACHER'S ROLE	STUDENT'S ROLE
Plans Assists in defining goals	Identifies ideas Sets goals
↓	↓
Creates positive classroom climate Suggests Challenges	Makes choices of work to be included Writes reasons for choices (self-reflection)
↓	↓
Conferences with student	Conferences with peers and teacher
↓	↓
Gives feedback	Receives feedback from peers and parents
↓	↓
Writes portfolio assessment Self-reflects and evaluates Plans curriculum	Defines strengths Defines areas of growth Sets new goals Self-assesses

EVALUATING PORTFOLIOS

We must address the question of evaluation: Should portfolios be graded? There are many schools of thought concerning the grading of portfolios. There is no right or wrong way, and the literature on this subject is voluminous. It is important to thoroughly examine the options and hold serious discussions with colleagues to determine your approach.

Endemic to portfolios is the notion that they serve as a self-assessment tool. If this is indeed the case, portfolios are undermined if the teacher assigns a grade to them. Why? Once the teacher assigns a grade, the portfolio shifts ownership from the student to the teacher. Grades are evaluative by nature, and by grading portfolios, we evaluate for the students rather then having students evaluate and reflect themselves.

There are some schools that have displaced grades with portfolios and provide a non-graded report card or report student progress using portfolios during parent conferences.

We must remember as we discuss this issue of grading portfolios that the work collected by students has already been evaluated by the teacher. When the individual pieces of work have been assessed, students overtly or covertly choose work that is meaningful based on their teachers' assessments.

Students can assess their own portfolios using the rubric on the following page.

A Rubric for
Evaluating My Portfolio

MY PORTFOLIO	LEVELS OF PERFORMANCE			
	3	2	1	0
Is complete				
Is organized				
Contains varied samples of written work				
Shows evidence of using many resources				
Shows evidence of problem-solving				
Shows evidence of decision making				
Shows evidence of higher-level thinking skills				
Includes examples of both individual and group work				
Includes self-reflective comments				
Reflects my enthusiasm for learning				
Contains many pieces that were not required or assigned				
Shows evidence of what I have learned				
Displays the pride I have in my work				
Shows maximum effort to reach my educational goals				
Is presented in a neat and orderly manner				

LEVELS OF PERFORMANCE:

3 = excellent   2 = good   1 = needs improvement   0 = missing

TEACHER SELF-REFLECTION

You have learned a lot about portfolios and hopefully have begun to develop and finalize a portfolio plan to use with your class. As students create portfolios that include serious self-reflection, it is a good idea for you as the teacher to undergo a similar experience. Review what you have done this year and reflect upon it so you can perfect it next year when you start the portfolio process again. Use the questions on the next page to help you reflect.

Self-Reflection
on My Portfolio Program

1. What subject areas were included? Would you change this?

_____

_____

2. Were you satisfied with the process for selecting content pieces for the portfolio? If not, what changes would you make?

_____

_____

3. Did the management system work for you? What did you like about it? What improvements would you make?

_____

_____

4. Were you satisfied with how the portfolio was shared? How would you improve this part of the program?

_____

_____

5. What did you learn from this process? What impact did it have on curriculum planning and on instructional strategies?

_____

_____

6. What is your overall assessment of the portfolio program you used this year? What suggestions for improvement do you have?

_____

_____

SOME QUESTIONS TO ASK YOURSELF ABOUT PORTFOLIO ASSESSMENT

This book may have prompted many thoughts, new ideas, and questions about how to assess your students' work. Take a moment and use the form on the following page to ask yourself how you can go forward now to put some of these ideas into practice.

As we end our discussion of assessing student work, we must always keep in mind that our goal is to recognize student progress and achievement. We must focus on the positive, on what students can do, not what they cannot do. We must continue to spend time self-reflecting upon what we are doing, how we are teaching, what we are teaching, and how we are evaluating what we are teaching. We must assess student work by looking at an assessment program which is directly linked to the standards established, the curriculum developed, and the instructional strategies used. When all of this is in place, we will have a comprehensive assessment program.

Some Questions to Ask Yourself about Portfolio Assessment

1. What are you now doing that prepares your students for the strategies and processes used in portfolio assessment?

_____

_____

_____

_____

_____

2. What are your concerns and staff development needs related to portfolio assessment?

_____

_____

_____

_____

_____

3. What one new strategy will you try in the next three months?

_____

_____

_____

_____

4. What are your next steps? What assistance do you need?

_____

_____

_____

_____

Glossary of Terms